DEANLAND A.L.G.

The History of a Sussex Airfield

By Peter Waring

My son, Nathan is really responsible for this book being written. His early interest in aircraft modelling and the RAF was stimulated by his finding a box of war time land mine detonators in our garden. This led to our seeking out the local Advanced Landing Ground situated at Deanland. Finding that no proper research had been carried out on its history, we set to work. Our research included unearthing not only a number of relics from around the airfield but also parts of four V1 bombs which landed in the area. We are most grateful to the many persons who related their memories of serving at Deanland or who lived in the area when the airfield was active, without which, much of the history recorded here would have been lost forever.

Revised Edition
2013

Published by Laughton Air Museum

ISBN 978-0-9526197-1-0

CONTENTS

Chapter   **Page**

   1. Advanced Landing Grounds............................ 1

   2. The RAF at Deanland................................. 7

   3. The Fight against Hitler's Revenge Weapons........ 12

   4. Action at Deanland................................. 16

   5. Deanland since the War.............................. 22

Appendix

   1. Squadron Details...................................... 26

   2. The Spitfires of Deanland............................. 29

   3. The A.L.G. specification for Deanland............. 31

   4. Other Local Airfields................................. 33

INTRODUCTION

Driving down the lane from Golden Cross to Ripe, a small village near Hailsham in East Sussex, there is little indication that, for a brief span of time, this was a place of action and drama. Most of what was Deanland Advanced Landing Ground has long since returned to agriculture. The woodland in which the tented accommodation was pitched is now a well known mobile home park and that part of the airfield still in use is hidden discreetly behind trees.

Deanland during the Second World War was a very different place. It's Squadrons were to play a varied but vital role in the fight for victory, their record of success fully in keeping with the proud record of the Royal Air Force. The airfield also had a number of unusual visitors, with many planes making emergency landings when damaged or short of fuel, Deanland being the first airfield they came upon after flying back over the English coast line.

The history of Deanland airfield does not stop with the end of the war. In the 1960's, the airfield was reborn and has developed under private ownership. It now has a number of small hangers and a wide range of aircraft types flown by the local enthusiasts.

CHAPTER ONE

Advanced Landing Grounds

Early in the war, the RAF was asking for additional airfields because of the risk of the comparatively few existing airfields being put out of action. Known as Emergency Landing Grounds (E.L.G.s), they were normally little more than grass surfaced fields.

In 1941, consideration was given to establishing more forward sites to enable the RAF to provide air support and fighter cover for a possible build up and landings on the European mainland in Operation Hadrian. This operation was postponed but 1942 saw the continuing search for what was now referred to as Advanced Landing Grounds (A.L.G.s). A.L.G.s were also to give an opportunity to tactical fighter squadrons to familiarise themselves with operating from airfields with only basic facilities which they could expect to be available to them on the European mainland after the invasion. Eventually, a total of 23 A.L.G.s were built.

The layout and the facilities for such landing grounds were decided upon. Each landing ground was to have two runways using Sommerfeld tracking. The main runway was to be 4,800 feet in length with a second runway, at ninety degrees to the main runway, to be of 4,200 feet. There was to be a perimeter tracking, hard standings for the aircraft and Blister hangers for undercover maintenance. Accommodation for billeting and support facilities was to be provided by tents with local housing being requisitioned where possible.

Deanland was one of two local sites surveyed in 1942 as possible location for an A.L.G., the other site being about three mile to the west at Shortgate, near Laughton. A letter from the Air Ministry, dated 13th June 1942, to East Sussex County Council, asking for their views on the acceptability of Shortgate and Deanland as sites for Advanced Landing Grounds concluded thus: 'As the service in question is to meet an urgent requirement and is vital to the efficient presentation of the war, I am to express the hope that no objection will be raised to the proposals.' A difficult request to refuse! On 15th September, the Air Ministry informed the County Council of their final choice, namely Deanland.

The area around Deanland was requisitioned under the Defence of the Realm Act in early 1943. Contractors for clearing the site, namely Len Page and his family from Golden Cross, moved in with their traction engines and steam winches. The traction engines had to be fired up and ready to start work by 8am each morning and they were paid for each tree they removed. For the more obstinate obstruction, dynamite was resorted to.

July 2nd 1943 saw the arrival of No.16 Airfield Construction Group of the Royal Engineers. The main runway was laid out running SE-NW and the second SW-NE. American Pierced Steel Planking (P.S.P.) was used on the taxiways with Bar and Rod Track, another American development, used at the marshalling areas.

Four blister hangers were erected and four 200 feet by 100 feet concrete standings laid for refuelling points. Small arms ammunition, pyrotechnic store and fuel storage sites were set up and sleeping sites cleared. No permanent buildings were constructed until July 1944 but the properties of Broadacres, Broomham Farm and Cleggetts Farm were requisitioned as Officer's quarters, the H.Q. and the armoury. The long list of other facilities stipulated to be provided at Deanland included was hard standing for the cooking area, air raid shelters and even the number of latrines, although these were little more than poles suspended over a trench. It was not until July that the few permanent buildings were erected, namely some mess huts and Nissan huts for sleeping quarters.

The airfield was officially opened on 1st April 1944 although it's existence was classified secret. The postal address was simply GPO Lewes.

Reaction to being posted to this rural backwater was somewhat mixed. S.H.Wilkinson, a member of the ground staff from April to August 1944 said, "They were good days, there under the Downs in what was a good summer even in the midst of war, and with the good comradeship that existed amongst us". Initial reaction from the incoming squadrons was somewhat different. Flight Officer G.C.McKay of No.91 Squadron carried out a recce prior to their arrival and found that facilities were extremely limited compared with their present posting at West Malling. He reported back the terrible news, concluding by saying, "It was the last place on earth any sane man would go to". However, it appears they settled in quickly, as, the day after their arrival, B Flight had a successful recce of Eastbourne, judging by the state of them on their return! The Green Man at Ringmer and the Golden Cross pub were to become popular watering holes as was the Crown Inn in Eastbourne. The main building of the Golden Cross pub was used by officers, the wooden extension at the rear, still there now, was built for 'other ranks'. There were also unofficial supplies of alcohol to be found at the airfield, with reports of quantities of red wine being stored in petrol cans.

Living under tents was a big comedown for most stationed at Deanland, or Tentland as it became known as. Certain enterprising ground crew, managed to improve their comfort by cutting sections from the Sommerfeld wire-mesh which they laid them over wooden uprights hammered into the ground, forming excellent mattresses. Food was generally considered rather poor. One pilot recalls that the best meal of the day was the eggs and toast cooked on a log fire washed down by some beer bought from the local pub. This was occasionally augmented by a chicken found 'lost' in the local countryside or a rabbit which had been caught. Sleeping under tents could be very cold and, during the period of the V1 attacks, the barrage put up by the local gun defences lead to many sleepless nights.

Deanland's time as an Advanced Landing Ground was short lived. Normandy was invaded and, as troops moved into France, the Spitfire squadrons moved forward in order to provide cover. Also, by the end of September, the menace of the V1 was over for the south of England. Deanland was officially closed in November. The tracking was removed by the Agricultural Committee although some Bar and Rod was still found locally at a farm in 1990, being used as field gates. The Sommerfeld tracking with it's mass of wire netting was dumped in the local woods. Much of the hard standing was dug up in 1946 and used as hardcore for a roadway leading to a sawmill, built shortly after the war by Laughton Estate in the nearby Laughton Forest. A downside of being so close to the airfield was they found many of the trees they were cutting up had cannon shells imbedded in them which damaged their band saws. The anti-glider posts from the adjacent fields which were dumped in the ditches were quickly recovered by the farmers and the local people for more domestic use! The lane joining Golden Cross with Ripe through the old airfield was not opened as a metalled road until August 1947, the previous route to Ripe being via Chalvington.

At one time, it appeared that another airfield existed in Laughton. An aerial photograph of the area taken in 1944 shows another apparent airstrip nearby in the Laughton Forest, in an area called the Devil's Race. This, in fact, was an area used by the Canadians in training to lay out airstrips. Having completed a runway, it was then bulldozed up again ready for the next training session. It was never operational although it was reported that an Auster and a Lysander did once land there. From the air, it must have looked an actual airfield as it was bombed once by German planes. A local resident, Tony Warbleton, recalled how, as a young boy, he had witnessed the bombing and thought that at least two of the bombs had not exploded. They are probably still there, deep in the soft ground.

The refuelling site near the north-west corner of the airfield is still clearly visible.

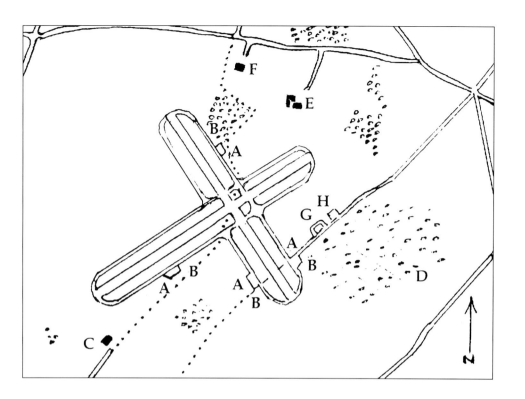

DEANLAND AIRFIELD

A. Refueling points
B. Blister Hangers
C. Armoury and Main Store (Cleggets Farm)
D. Sleeping quarters (Deanland Woods)
E. Squadron Office, Briefing room, H.Q. and PBX (Broomham Farm)
F. Officers Quarters (Broadacres)
G. Petrol store
H. Oil Store

Cleggetts Farm stood at what is now the entrance to the present airfield. The ground floor was used as the armoury, the barn and outbuildings as stores.

The Summerfeld tracking used for the runways were torn up after the war and, it appears, much of it dumped in the local woods judging by the quantity still found around.

Aerial view of Deanland A.L.G clearly shows the perimeter track around the runways. (A22 runs top right, the road from Golden Cross to Deanland runs diagonally down left).

CHAPTER TWO

The RAF at Deanland

Spitfire Mk. LFVB (BM 594) belonging to No. 611 Squadron while at Deanland.

It was April 1944 before RAF Squadrons finally flew into Deanland. No. 131 Polish Airfield, 84 Group of the 2nd Tactical Air Force, led by Wing Commander Zbigniew Czaykowski, was formed from Polish personnel who had escaped from the continent after the German invasion. The reputation of the Polish aircraft men as exceptionally determined pilots had been firmly established in the Battle of Britain. Their country had already been occupied by Germany and they had a passionate desire to fight back. Consisting of No's 302, 308 and 317 Squadrons, it moved into Deanland on 1st April. The day of their arrival was not without incident as a Mustang called in just before they landed and collided with the wind sock.

Their arrival coincided with a period of cold and overcast weather with flying only possible once in the next five days. Even then, this, their first real operation from Deanland, with four aircraft sent on a Ranger mission over France, had to be abandoned just before their aircraft reached the French coast, owing to the weather. The day finished with two accidents. Flt.Sgt Pilarek, of No. 302 Squadron, flying Spitfire MH842, was seriously injured when his aircraft stalled on his final turn and crashed into woods south of the SW/NE runway. And then, Flt.Sgt. Skupinski, of the same squadron, crashed his Spitfire (MH 313) at Allanfield Farm, Chiddingly, only ten minutes after taking off. Huddled in such weather in their tented accommodation, it was depressing start to their stay at Deanland.

Flying Mk.IX Spitfires, three-quarters of which were newly configured as fighter/bombers, they carried out training exercises in their new role. They also were sent on Ramrod sorties over France, acting as cover for mainly Marauders and Bostons. They carried out the occasional

'Ranger' mission, described as deep-penetration flights to engage targets of opportunity and also took part in Air Sea Rescue operations. 22nd April saw No.308 Squadron loaded with 500 pound bombs for the first time, all returning successful after hitting their targets in France.

No.302 Squadron moved out briefly on 12th April to Southend for armament and bombing training and practice. They continued dive bombing and air to ground firing practice until the afternoon of 14th April when they returned to Deanland. They then had to wait another four days before weather conditions permitted further flying!

During their stay at Deanland, the Squadrons were visited by General Sosnkowski, the Polish Air Force Commander in Chief together with the Commander of the Allied Expeditionary Air Force, Air Chief Marshal Trafford Leigh Mallory and the head of the 2nd TAF, Air Chief Marshall 'Maori' Cunningham. Distinguished visitors indeed!

The Polish airfield stayed only a short time. No's 302 and 317 Squadrons moved to another Advanced Landing Ground which had been constructed at Chailey, to the north of Lewes. No.308 Squadron joined them two days later. They were to remain at Chailey over D-Day when they were to provide low level cover over the Normandy beaches. The flexibility required of squadrons at that period of the war is shown in the number of moves the Polish squadrons had to make. From Chailey, No.131 Airfield moved to Appledrum on 28th June, then to Ford on 16th July and on 4th August, they moved across to France.

No.149 Airfield, 11 Group ADGB, moved to Deanland on 29th April with No.234 Squadron, flying Mk.VI Spitfires and No.64 Squadron with Mk.Vc Spitfires. No. 611 Squadron with Mk. Vb Spitfires joined them on 30th April. Their role at Deanland was to provide escorts for Mitchells and Bostons of No.2 Group and for B26 Marauders of the IX AF which were employed on softening up the Atlantic Wall defences. For example, on 2nd May No.234 Squadron accompanied 72 Maurauders attacking the railway marshalling yards at Valenciennes. On 15th May, the designation 'Airfield' was changed to a new term, 'Wing'. Thus No.149 Airfield became known as No.149 Wing.

At the beginning of May, all three squadrons were involved in Exercise Fabius. This was a full dress rehearsal for the invasion and took place between Littlehampton and Shoreham. The Spitfires practiced pre-dawn take offs before flying low-level cover, a role they would undertake over the beaches of Normandy. As facilities for night flying were limited at Deanland, the sorties were carried out from Tangmere. More local training occurred at Eastbourne baths where they practised their dinghy skills in the event of them having to ditch in the sea.

On 4th June, orders came through for invasion markings to be painted on all aircraft. Ground crew and pilot's enthusiasm to apply 18 inch wide black and white stripes were hampered by the torrential rain that fell in the evening. The stripes had to be reapplied the following day. The three squadrons were called together by Wing Commander L.A.Powell, who outlined the plan of attack. The airfield was placed under armed guard and all personnel confined to the airfield until further notice.

D-Day saw the airfield at full stretch over the Normandy beach head. No.611 Squadron was airborne at 3.48 hours and was the first British squadron to be over the invasion beaches of Gold and Omaha. They were able to spend 50 minutes over the beaches before they had to head back. No's 64 and 234 Squadrons took off at 5.20am. Each squadron carried out 4 patrols that day. This hectic schedule continued for the next few days, putting an enormous strain on the ground crew to keep the aircraft serviceable and the pilots to endure the wearing effects of constant operations. This was not helped by the increasing number of V1s appearing after D- Day with the barrage put up by the local ground defences leading to many a sleepless night.

There was little activity from the Luftwaffe in the first few days; their main preoccupation was to avoid being shot down by naval gunfire or American Air Force planes and avoiding anti-aircraft balloons flying from the invasion fleet. The first German aircraft they shot down was on 10th June, a Ju.88, achieved by No.611 Squadron Leader, Sqn. Ldr. W.A. Douglas.

The exploits of the three squadrons over this period are deserving a book on it's own. However, it is worth recorded one particular event which will give some indication of the pressures they were working under.

Relating to Spitfires of No.234 Squadron, it was the 14th June and they were patrolling between Bayeux and Caen. On their second run along the line, they came under heavy anti-aircraft fire. Three were hit and their pilots Flt.Lt. 'Johnny' Johnston, Flt.Off. Bill Painter and Flt.Sgt. Joe Fargher had to make emergency landings. Fortunately, they came down close to an Army airfield construction unit who provided them with a car and driver to take them to the coast. Arriving at a functioning airfield, they were confronted by Air Vice Marshall Harry Broadhurst demanding what they were doing there. However, another officer approached them, none other than Sir Trafford Leigh-Mallory, Air Chief Marshal, AOC in C, Allied Expeditionary Air Force who also was visiting the site together with members of the Press Corp. Seeing this as an excellent publicity opportunity, he had photographs of the three pilots taken in front of his personal Dakota before taking them back with him to Thorney Island.

The next morning, the three pilots were flown back to Deanland and, that same afternoon, they were again on operational duty over Normandy! Sadly, Bill Painter was killed three days later by 'friendly' fire over Beachy Head. Both he, in Spitfire BL720 and Flt.Off. George Sparrow in EN 861 were fired at by AA guns. Taking evasive action, the two Spitfires collided and crashed. Only Flt.Off. Sparrow survived.

No's 64 and 234 Squadron were escorting tugs and gliders of No.38 Group to their drop zones for the 6th Airborne Division during the initial stages of operation Overlord and later carried out missions against German positions.

Another example of the pressure they were working under was on 7th June when Tony Cooper, flying back very late in appalling weather and 10/10 cloud, managed to locate the airfield when they fired Very Lights up. His fuel ran out as he landed.

Lt. Mike Bernard , a Free French pilot flying with No.234 Squadron, was to lose his Spitfire in unusual circumstances. On patrol near Cain, his aircraft suffered some flak damage. He decided to make a precautionary landing on a coastal road. As soon as the local farmers saw his French uniform, he was feted as a returning hero and carried off shoulder high for a celebratory drink.... or two. Returning later to where he had landed, he found that his aircraft had disappeared. The British Army had found it blocking the road and had simply dumped it off the side of the cliff. Explain that to your Commanding Officer!

The three squadrons of No.149 Wing moved out of Deanland between 19th and 26th June, No's 64 and 611 to Harrowbeer and No.234 to Predannack. This transfer was performed by No.575 Squadron using their 17 Dakotas to transport all the personnel and equipment. Considering the work load No.234 Squadron had undertaken, Squadron Engineering Officer Tony Credon reported that all bar one of their 24 Spitfires were able to fly that day to Predannack. This reflected very well on the ground crew who had had to operate in one of the most hectic periods in the R.A.F.'s history.

It was not until 21st July that the airfield was again occupied. No's 91 and 322 Squadrons of 85 Group 2nd TAF, flying Mk.XIV Spitfires, moved in to continue their 'anti-diver' role, attacking V1 flying bombs. To help increase the aircraft speed in order to gain on the faster V1s, the Browning machine guns had been removed and the ground crew kept the aircraft highly polished.

No.91 Squadron had a nickname of 'Jim Crow' through their frequent duties previously of doing coastal reconnaissance patrols. Tragedy hit their squadron on 15th August when their Squadron Leader, Norman Arthur Kynaston DFC and bar was killed. He had a fine record, shooting down four enemy aircraft plus one shared claim, one probable and one damaged. He also had a tally of 17 V1s shot down. The circumstances of his death are not known.

No.322 Squadron was mainly Dutch pilots. They were to suffer a loss on 18th September when Flt.Off. L.D.Wolters crashed at Kenardington, Kent.

A third squadron joined them on 16th August, No. 345 Free French Squadron with their Mk.Vb Spitfires. They suffered their first casualty there on 18th September when Spitfire PT 913 went missing over the Channel. There was no sign of the pilot or the aircraft. It was presumed he had ditched.

By the end of August, the main onslaught of the V1s was over. The Spitfires of No's 91 and 322 Squadron were changed in late August to Mk.IXs.

September 1st was a dramatic day for the leaders of No.322 Squadron. Squadron Leader Major K.C. Kulmann was hit by flak over France and had to bale out. He landed safely but was captured. Flight Commanders Flt.Lt.Van Eendenburg and Flt.Lt.Plesman were also hit by flack. Flt.Lt. Plesman crashed at St Omer and was killed. Flt.Lt Van Eendenburg also crashed and not only survived but managed to return to Britain on 12th September. He was subsequently promoted to Squadron Leader of No.322 (Dutch) Squadron, it's first Dutch commander.

The three squadrons were to stay until October, carrying out day bomber raids and armed reconnaissance operations. After the 10th October 1944, there was no further RAF activity at Deanland, the airfield being officially closed in November.

A Mk LF IXE Spitfire of No.322 Squadron at Deanland. Pictured here, is Princess Juliana of the Netherlands speaking to Sqn. Ldr C.M.van Eedenborg on her visit to the airfield in September 1944.

SQUADRON ACES

No. 302 Squadron
Flt. Lt. Stanislaw Brzeski V.M.F. C.V. + 4 bars D.F.C.
Claims – destroyed 7 plus 3 shared, probable 4, damaged 1 plus
 1 observation balloon destroyed and 1 aircraft destroyed on the ground.

No. 308 Squadron
Capt. Witold Rettinger
Claims – destroyed 4, damaged 4.

No. 64 Squadron
Sqn. Ldr. John Noble MacKenzie (New Zealander)
Claims – destroyed 6, probable 4, damaged 2.

No. 91 Squadron
Sqn. Ldr Norman Arthur Kynaston D.F.C. + bar
Claims – destroyed 4 plus 1 shared, probable 1, damaged 1.

No.611 Squadron
Sqn. Ldr Bill Douglas D.F.C
Claims – 6 destroyed.

CHAPTER THREE

The Fight Against Hitler's Revenge Weapon

June 1944 saw the start of Hitler's Revenge Weapon onslaught on Britain. It was on 23rd June that German radio was first heard to refer to the Vergeltungswaffen Ein (V1). It was a pilotless, pre-aimed monoplane powered by a pulse jet. It's petrol engine was fed by compressed air. Flying between 3000 and 4000 feet at speeds between 250 and 400mph, it carried a bomb load of 850kg of high explosive. Initially called a pilotless aircraft (PAC), it's official existence was not confirmed by the Ministry of Home Security until after 20th June 1944 when the Cabinet decided that, in future, the PAC should be referred to as the Flying Bomb (FB). This was because they feared that the public would panic at the thought of pilotless aircraft attacking them. It came also to be called the doodlebug or buzz-bomb; it's official code name was diver.

The range of the V1 was about 130 miles. Hence to strike London, the launch sites had to be in the Pas de Calais. Often they would not reach their target and would fall short on what was to become known as Doodlebug Alley. Deanland was right in this flight path. The first V1 to land in Sussex, and only the second reported in the country, was at Mizbrook Farm, Cuckfield, at 4.20am on 13th June. Shortly after, a V1 crashed at Ticehurst without exploding, enabling the authorities to examine the first example they had of the flying bomb. The period of V1 strikes was mainly over by September by which time 886 had landed on the county.

To avoid the problem of our aircraft being hit by AA guns while both were firing at the V1s, formal orders went out on 17th July forbidding the fighters to attack the V1s along the coast from Cuckmere Haven, just to the west of Eastbourne, to St. Margarets Bay, which lies between Dover and Deal. This coastal border was 10,000 yards out to sea to 6,000 yards inland and at any height up to 8,000 feet.

The Tempest, with it's greater speed, was the most successful aircraft against V1s. The less powerful Mk. XIV Spitfires of 91 Squadron, with a top speed of 395 mph, had great difficulty in catching their targets, thus a stern chase was not possible. To help the aircraft fly faster, any inessentials were stripped off to reduce weight. This would include armour plating which normally protected the pilot from enemy fire. The most successful technique was for the pilot, alerted by Radar Stations or the Observer Corps, would fly a parallel course of the V1, allowing the craft to overtake him. They would then open fire at an oblique angle, preferably not closer than 200 yards to avoid damage to the aircraft should the V1 blow up. This happened to Flight Officer George McKinley of No 611 Squadron, just prior to their transfer to Deanland, when he fired at a V1 over Seaford. The V1 exploded, causing McKinley to lose control, crash and be killed.

A way the pilot was able to achieve a greater speed was to dive on to the V1 from above. However, this could be hazardous for people on the ground as, when the pilot fired, his guns were effectively being aimed at the ground. A farmer working in a field in Chiddingly, just north of Deanland, had his horse shot and his hay tedder damaged in such an incident.

No's 91 and 322 Squadron began their anti-diver roles when based at West Malling. Moving to Deanland on 21st July, they continued their successful role. It was a pilot of No.91 Squadron, Flying Officer Ken Collier, who first employed the technique of tipping a V1. Being short of ammunition, he put his own wing under the wing of the V1, causing the flying bomb to crash prematurely. Whilst this technique saved many lives at the intended destination of the V1, there were sometimes tragic results. On 7th July, a V1 was tipped at Polegate resulting in four deaths on the ground. Another V1 was tipped on 23rd July over Lower Dicker killing two people in Camberlot Road. The price for defending London was high! However, there was some consolation in that only 25% of the rockets reached their target, the remainder failing because of malfunction, a faulty giro system or being destroyed by aircraft or AA guns.

Three pilots of No.91 Squadron were killed while attacking V1s while at Deanland. On 26th July, Pilot Eugene Seghers flying Spitfire RM743 attacked a V1 at a ninety degree angle, lost sight of it and then collided with it. Both aircraft exploded., the aircraft crashing at Wares Pottery, Ridgewood, Uckfield. Another collision occurred on 31st July between Pilot Officer Paddy Schade in his Spitfire (RM 654) and Flt.Sgt. A.A.Wilson flying a Tempest (EJ 586) when both attacked the same V1. Paddy Schades crashed at Sandhurst Lane, Bexhill and A.A.Wilson at Halsea Farm, Hooe.

The third pilot to die from No.91 Squadron was Captain Jean Maridor. Attacking a V1 in his Spitfire (RM 656) he fired , hitting it's tail. Realising that the V1 would crash on a hospital, he attacked again but came too close. The V1 exploded, blowing the wing off his aircraft and crashed into a field near Benenden, Kent. Captain Maridor was due to be married the following week in Oxford to Jean Lambourne. A model of a Spitfire and a V1 had been made ready to put on the wedding cake.

Records of other V1s being shot down locally include one on 5th July at Terrible Down, 2 miles north west of Deanland. It caused damage to three dwellings but no one was injured. On 29th July, one was shot at over Laughton, exploding in mid-air. The remains fell on Blackshaw Wood. The explosion damaged the Parish church, the Vicarage and a number of other buildings. A day later, Sqn.Ldr. P.M.Bond of No.91 Squadron shot down a V1 over Whitesmith. The Squadron Diarist noted 'had the indecency to shoot a Diver down within half a mile of the aerodrome. Too close for comfort, was the general opinion!'

A further V1 fell at Plaquet Corner, Arlington, two miles south east of the airfield on 17th July. On 23rd July, another was shot down, exploding by Camberlot Road, a mile to the east, completely wrecking a house on Camberlot Home Farm and causing six casualties. Yet another V1 was shot down over Lower Vert Wood on 6th August, again within half a mile from the Airfield. It exploded on landing leaving a crater 8 foot deep, 20 feet in diameter. There were no casualties. An 8 foot section of this V1 was excavated from this site in 1995.

Finally, a sad local story is regard to one of the last V1s to land in the county. Flying past Deanland, its wings snagged a barrage balloon cable flying near Halland, some three miles north west of the airfield. The V1 swung back and crashed on the hamlet of Shortgate, near Laughton, destroying three houses, one of which was the sub-post office. Five people were killed including the post mistress and the visiting butcher on his deliveries from Ringmer.

Achieving 185 kills with their Spitfires, No.91 Squadron had the third highest score of all squadrons against V1s with No.32 Squadron coming fifth with 108 kills. The two most successful squadrons, namely No's 3 and 486 Squadrons, achieving scores of 357 and 223 respectively, were flying the more powerful Tempests.

Collecting pieces of V1s was a popular interest of many a schoolboy and also the occasional grown up. Mr Noakes, a local cattle dealer, picking up a particularly jagged piece of bomb, was heard to comment, "This jagged edge could cut your bloody hand off!" The Germans may have commented; ' well, that's the purpose of the bomb!'

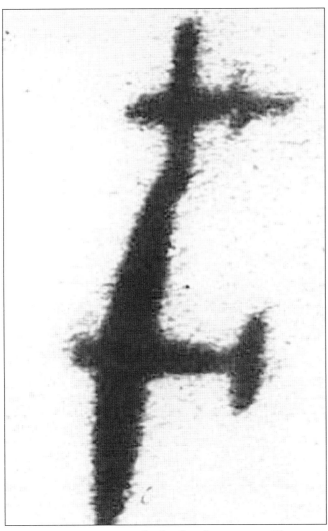

Dramatic picture of a Spitfire about to tip a V1

V1 Aces at Deanland

The following records are of pilots of No's 91 and 322 Squadrons who achieved 4 or more V1 kills whist with their squadron.

No.91 Squadron

Sqn. Ldr. N.A.Kynaston D.F.C. and bar	17
Flt.Off. R.S.Nash	16½
Flt.Off. E.Topham	15
Capt. J.M.Maridor	11
Flt.Off. J.A.Johnson	11
Flt.Off. Cruikshank	9½
Flt.Lt. P.M.Bond	9
Flt.Off. F. De Bordas	8½
Flt.Off. W.C.Marshall D.F.C.	8½
Flt.Off. A.R.L.Elcock	8
Flt.Lt. H.B.Moffett	7
Flt.Off. R.A.McPhie	6½
Flt.Off. K.R.Collier	6
Sqn. Ldr. J.W.O.Draper	6
Flt.Off. J.A.Faulkner	5½

No. 322 Squadron

Flt.Off. R.F.Burgwal	21
Flt.Off. J.van Arbel	12
Flt.Off. J.L.Plesman	12
Flt.Off. G.F.J.Jongbloed	9½
Sqn.Ldr.C.M.van Eedenborg	8
Flt.Sgt. M.J.Janssen	6
Flt.Sgt. R.L.Van Beers	5

CHAPTER 4

Action at Deanland

Aviation was an early arrival to the area. In 1912, an airfield was built at St. Antony's Hill, Eastbourne and, a year later a seaplane factory was built at the Crumbles. During the First World War, the Eastbourne Aerodrome had become one of the busiest and most important R.N.A.S flying schools in the country. In 1915, there was another air base created by the R.N.A.S. at Polegate, this time for it's airships. It was there that the first ever experiments with parachutes took place.

Slightly more locally, an airfield was established at Wilmington. Opened during the First World War, Wilmington was designated a Home Defence Landing Ground. However, it was little used until 1932 when the Sussex Aero Club was established there. Their first aircraft were some De Havilland 60G Moths used for pilot training.

In 1935 the Aero Club closed and the Eastbourne Flying Club formed, it's opening ceremony being performed by Amy Johnson. The airfield flourished in the next few years. There was even the suggestion that it should become the Eastbourne Municipal Airport! Minister of Transport, Leslie Hoare-Belisha learnt to fly here; and under the Air Ministry 'Civil Air Guard Scheme', flying lessons were offered through the local Labour Exchange, to anyone aged 18 to 50 aspiring to become a pilot. Training time for a pilot in those days was seven to eight actual flying hours!

An 'At Home Day' was held in 1935 with flying demonstrations from a Cantelever Pon and a Pobjoy Swallow. Among the aircraft on display were also a Monospar Ambulance and a Leopard Moth. The same event next year attracted over 72 aircraft, including a number of German pilots. The 1938 At Home Day included the first fighting machines to be seen at Wilmington when No.79 Squadron flew in from Biggin Hill with their Gloster Gauntlets. Other aircraft on display that day were a Mew Gull and a Messerschmitt M35, it's tail emblazoned with a swastika! It was flown by the renowned German aerobatic pilot, Vera Von Bissing.

The 1919 Treaty with Germany banned their designing and making of military aircraft so the German aircraft industry had taken to making so-called sports aircraft to help them develop and test ideas and components for any future military machine.

Despite the approaching war, an At Home Day still went ahead on 12th August 1939 but closed almost immediately after on 3rd September with the outbreak of war. The airfield was bombed early in the war by a low flying Dornier DO215, the explosion throwing a large quantity of mud over the A27, temporarily closing the road. There is no record of the Air Ministry considering this as a military airfield again as with a grass strip measuring 400 yards by 350 yards, it was no way a large enough area as a site for an Advanced Landing Ground. Although the airfield was never used again, the old club house and tower was not, in fact demolished until 1970.

Closer to home but before the airfield at Deanland was established, there are a number of records of aircraft making unscheduled landings. On 21st September 1940, a Lysander (R9003) of No.110 Squadron, piloted by Flight Officer Chandler, made a forced landing when short of fuel, one mile north of Ripe. (This aircraft is still in existence and is on display at Canada's Space and Aviation Museum.) Also in a similar proximity, a Spitfire MkVb (BS123) of No.402 Squadron, piloted by Pilot Officer Magee, crash landed, due to a technical fault, on 24th August 1942. Three Hurricanes are also recorded to have crashed locally. On 13th September 1940, one crashed at Perryland Wood, Chiddingly, another at Whigligh Wood, East Hoathly on 1st December 1940 and a third at Stream Farm, Chiddingly on 18thMarch 1941. This third Hurricane, piloted by Sgt Hughes of No.17 Squadron, had been attacked by a flight of Messerschmidtt 109's. His aircraft dived vertically into a field but he managed to bale out and land safely. Another Hurricane from the same squadron was hit in this incident and crashed at Blackboys. Sgt. Bartlett, the pilot, also managing to bail out safely.

Two days after the first of the two Sommerfeld runways had been completed at Deanland, in August 1943, a wounded Spitfire pilot put down at the airfield. No other details of this incident are known. The first aircraft to make a scheduled landing at Deanland was an Avro Anson, bringing in officials to inspect the newly completed airfield.

On 16th September 1943, a much more notable event occurred when a large number of B17s returning from a mission over Germany, landed at Deanland. Only recently has a report of this incident been discovered published in a 1943 issue of Life Magazine. Entitled 'Any landing you walk away from is a good one', it was written by their reporter, Frank T. Scherschel, who was onboard one of these aircraft. Subsequently, the full story of the raid leading to this incident has been uncovered.

Destination, the Robert Bosch factories in Stuttgart, 19 B17s of 303rd BG(H) took off from Molesworth, each loaded with 10 x 500 bombs, ammunition for their own guns and packets of leaflets to drop. Two aircraft had to abort the mission, leaving 17 to reach the target. However, 10/10 cloud cover obscured the target. The formation circled the city for 10 minutes before dropping their bombs. Flak over the target was moderate to intense and fairly accurate. From 50 to 100 enemy fighters were seen and were attacking the formation all the way to the target and back out. One report said, 'It could have been a lot worse but those gunners of ours just raised hell with those fighters'. Six enemy aircraft were destroyed with another 5 probables claimed. With the delay in dropping their bombs and the twisting and weaving to put off the aim of the anti-aircraft guns, many of the aircraft were running short of fuel with only 5 making it back to Molesworth. The Old Squaw (42-3002 427BS) ran out of fuel over the Channel and crashed 6 miles southwest of Beachy Head. The crew were recovered by Air-Sea Rescue based at Newhaven. Ten of the remaining aircraft put down at the first airfield they came to, namely Deanland. The original confusion on the numbers can be understood when one reads the eye witness account of the Life Magazine reporter; 'All about us, planes were landing in all directions, upwind, downwind'. It was this that caused the eleventh B17, Winning Run 42-29944 to crash at Deanland. To make it so far, they had already jettisoned ammunition, radio equipment and anything else removable.

Coming into land on his first approach, Pilot Jacob James had to take emergency evasive action to avoid hitting another B17 coming in to land from a different direction. In doing so, his last engine ran out of fuel and the plane crash landed, ending up across the Chalvington Road. Three of it's crew were injured but managed to get out of the plane. It's undercarriage was broken off and the aircraft was declared a total loss. Being outside the perimeter of the airfield, it allowed a number of local schoolboys to get close up to investigate and the crew even lifted some of them on board to look around.

The terror and relief of the reporter can be felt in a wonderfully descriptive paragraph from his story. 'We landed on a wing with four engines dead. My prayers had all been said going into south-west Germany. We wished ourselves out of Germany, cursed the Nazi fighters through France, said a prayer for our gas to hold out to the Channel and thanked God or His Son for the sight of the English coastline. We crash landed in a pasture after missing two houses.'

Another incident involving a B17 occurred on 6th November when 2nd Lt William Holden landed his aircraft at Deanland also short of fuel after a raid over Germany.

On 4th March 1944, a Mustang of No.336 Squadron piloted by Lt Jack l. Raphael put down when short of fuel as his right wing fuel tank would not draw. On 17th May 1944, a Tempest V (JN762) of No.3 Squadron was damaged whilst landing at Deanland. Another B.17F to land at Deanland was on 4th June, 1944 when Lt Raymond J Tombley flying Star Duster 42-97193 put down at the airfield his aircraft badly damaged and one of his engines out of action. He had been hit by friendly fire over the Channel. It is understood he came into land whist they were repairing the runway. Red Very lights were fired to warn him off but the pilot ignored them and landed, only to slew off onto soft ground. As the aircraft still had it's bomb load on, they had to jack the aircraft up to get at the bombs before they could actually recover the aircraft. Finally, the aircraft was pulled back onto firm ground with the help of four caterpillar tractors and it's own engines.

The airfield was unexpectedly filled to capacity on 8th June 1944 when the Mk Vb Spitfires of No.350 Squadron (Belgian), led by Wg Com Don Kingaby, flew in for a night stop over, when their own base at Friston, near Beachy Head, became unserviceable. This squadron was also on patrol over the Normandy beaches on D-Day

On 12th July 1944 Capt Robert T Harris, returning from a mission over France, landed his B26 Marauder 386BG 553BS. On 20th July 1944 another Tempest (EJ527) of No.486 Squadron (NZ) made a forced landing after engine failure, at Stone Cross Farm, Laughton, just to the west of the airfield. The pilot, Warrant Officer S.J.Short was injured, the aircraft written off. And on the 21st July, a B.24 Liberator 392BG 579BS crashed at Deanland, finishing up close to the officers quarters at Broadacres. Other aircraft known to have put down at Deanland were a Thunderbolt, a Walrus, a Mustang and a Lightning. The P47D Lightning,(42-75614) piloted by Stanley Stepniz, made it's mark when the brakes failed on landing and it took out part of the hedge at the south end of the NE/SW runway. On 21st August, Lt Benson piloting B.24F 42-51212 crash landed at the airfield, ripping his left undercarriage off. The salvage team from 3rd Strategic Air Depot, based in Wotton, Norfolk, moved in the next day to recover it.

A regular visitor was a Dragon Rapide, bringing in mail and squadron's orders. Deanland was also visited by Douglas Dakotas of Nos.271and 575 Squadrons, part of Transport Command. These squadrons were tasked with moving equipment and supplies when fighter squadrons moved base. One of the pilots was the later famed comedian, Jimmy Edwards. His visit was evidenced with his signature, together with other pilots of his squadron, being found on a ceramic tile at Broadacres, the officer's quarters.

A perpetual problem at Deanland during the summer occurred when the ground dried out. The steel pickets which held the Sommerfeld tracking in place would ride up with the weight of the planes going over. This could prove very hazardous for the next plane to land. Thus the knocking of pickets back into the ground became a continuous chore. The nature of the tracking caused other problems. A DH82A Tiger Moth T6309 was damaged on landing when it's tail skid got caught in the netting. When the netting rode up, it tended to tear the tyres to ribbons.

Princess Juliana of the Netherlands made a formal visit to No.322 Squadron (Dutch) on 26th September 1944 and was introduced to all the pilots and ground crew. Prince Bernard of the Netherlands also visited, flying in in his Spitfire to visit the squadron. Unfortunately he made a heavy landing and burst a tyre.

Supporting the airfield were a battery of Bofor guns and searchlights, the latter being based one in Ripe and the second just south of Laughton Church.

There is a lovely story of some boys who found an aircraft target and 300 feet of rope at Abbots Wood, a two miles east of Deanland. Their conscience led them to return the target to Deanland. However, their reception by the Polish Air Force guards was rather frightening. Growled at in a strange foreign language, they were marched off to the guard room where they were locked in. They were fearful of what was to happen to them but ten minutes later, the door was opened by a beaming guard laden with sandwiches, sausage rolls, jam tarts and cold drinks. There followed a VIP tour of the airfield, before finally, friendly farewells were said.

Other stories related to aircraft in the area are worth recording. Two miles north of Deanland, the field beside Rowland Wood was used by up to 5 Austers for a number of weeks leading up to the invasion. It is believed they were a detachment from No. 657 Squadron Air Observation Corp based at that time at East Grinstead. They were using this forward landing strip to be closer to the beaches of Normandy for Operation Overlord. The pilots and ground crew were billeted in the East Hoathly Village Hall.

In the nearby town of Hailsham, the timber company, Green Brothers, were producing full size replica Hurricane aircraft. Some five hundred of these Hurricanes were made for the RAF on their 'K sites'. These were day time decoys simulating satellite airfields, usually equipped with false buildings, movements and aircraft.

Finally, two stories of local bombing incidents. At nearby Laughton Lodge Hospital, the gardeners and patients had one morning being digging out tree stumps to enlarge the area for growing vegetables. During their lunch break, the field was bombed, effectively removing all the tree stumps for them! The down side was that it also destroyed the vegetables they had been growing. Laughton Lodge also supported the war effort by recycling the empty tin cans from the hospital. When sufficient had been collected, they were placed on the road for the local steam roller to crush them before being loaded up and taken away.

On another occasion, local resident, Mrs Booth of Averys Oak, Laughton, was particularly incensed by a high explosive bomb landing near by, not only because it damaged the roof of her house, it also destroyed her meat safe into which she had just put a brawn to set!

PARISH CHURCH
LAUGHTON
VICTORY
Thanksgiving Service
SUNDAY, August 19th. 1945.

NATIONAL ANTHEM
THE BIDDING   Mr. John Heys
THANKSGIVINGS
HYMN 298.....Praise, my Soul, the King
SOLO   Miss Ough
O had I Jubal's Lyre (from Handel)
PSALM 136. (The Great 'HALLEL')
O give Thanks unto the LORD
ISAIAH 54, vv 10 to 17.
General Hanbury
PSALM 67 (Deus Misereatur)
GOD be merciful unto us
REVELATIONS 21, vv 1 to 7.
Pte. D. Brett
THE CREED and PRAYERS
2 KINGS 19, vv 10 to 19, & 35 to 37.
Mr. E. Shoosmith
HYMN.........Through the Night of Doubt
SERMON...............'The New Star'
The Rev. J. Ough M.A.
HYMN..............The Supreme Sacrifice
THE BLESSING
THE DOXOLOGY

Copy of the Victory Service held at the local Parish Church in Laughton on 19th August 1945

The B17 'Winning Run' which crashed at Deanland on 16th September 1943. Yet another B17 appears to be coming in to land.

The B24 which crash landed at Deanland on 21st August 1944

CHAPTER 5

Deanland since the War

The name Deanland is now associated mainly with the beautiful woodland setting of a park for modern mobile homes. This occupies the southern edge of Deanland Wood where one of the Blister hangers had once stood. The car park at the Deanland Wood Park was the refuelling area for aircraft. Most of the evidence of the actual wartime airfield has disappeared with only a few concrete standings still visible.

In the 1950s, Deanland Wood, where the tented accommodation had been pitched, was for a while a nudist colony.

The present airfield of Deanland is located a half mile south of Deanland Wood Park, being situated on what was the southern end of the S.W./N.E. runway. After the war, this area, which had returned to agricultural use, was owned by Mr. Frank Ferral. Following his death, the land was sold on again to Mr Richard Chandless.

The first task Mr Chandless set himself was to improve the farmland. He found there was still some Sommerfeld tracking in place which was not easy too move, being now well matted into the grass. Even more of the problem was that many of the steel stakes used to fix the track to the ground, had been left in the ground. About three tons of various tracking components ware eventual extracted. A further problem arose when ploughing with live 20mm cannon shells being turned up. Closer investigation revealed that they had uncovered a large arms cash of 200-300 rounds of 20mm cannon shells and several thousand rounds of 0.303 bullets. Some over zealous quartermaster had obviously decided to bury his excess stock.

Mr Chandless had always been interested in aircraft and this interest was further aroused by a friend who had learnt to fly and started to use the strip at Deanland, although there was no runway, just field. After obtaining his pilots licence, Mr Chandless purchased his own plane, a French built Emeralde (CP 301A). This he first kept at Shoreham but his enthusiasm for flying led him to lay out a runway 457 x 27 metres at Deanland in the early 1960s. After constructing a small hanger, he moved his aircraft over. Mr Chandless's interest in flying grew and he became an agent for the French aircraft manufacturer, CES (Centre Est Aeronautique). Interest in the airfield also grew. The next plane to be based there was a Turbulent owned by Mr Roy Brook. With the nearest airfields on the South Coast being Lydd in Kent and Shoreham in West Sussex, others also expressed a wish to base their aircraft more locally at Deanland.

In the late 1960s, a brief drama occurred at Deanland. Shoreham airport at that time used to hold the King's Cup Air Race at their annual Air Show. During a practice run for the race, a heavy sea fog rolled in unexpectedly and the aircraft had to put down in a hurry at the nearest airfield. It is reported that fifteen aircraft landed at Deanland in nine minutes!

The two largest aircraft known to have landed at the airstrip since the war were a Piper Navajo and a Britten Norman Islander.

A busy Deanland Airfield at the 'fly in' in 2013.

Vintage planes still call in to Deanland. Here a Tiger Moth, one of the members of the Tiger Club which flew in on the 50th anniversary of the airfield.

The Golden Cross Public House, the 'local' to Deanland Airfield. Only Officers used the main building. The timber room at the rear was erected for 'other ranks'.

The entrance to Deanland Wood Park, once a refuelling area for the Spitfires and the site of a blister hanger. The runway ran immediately south of the car park.

In 1992, the airfield was sold to Mr Gerry Price, Mr David Brook and Mr Roy Brook. By this time there were two main hangers and around ten aircraft based there. Surprisingly, true legitimacy did not come to Deanland until March 1994 when Wealden District Council planning committee agreed to issue a certificate making the use of the airfield official.

On the 4th, 5th and 6th June 1994, the 50th anniversary of the landings at Deanland was commemorated throughout the country. On the 4th and 5th, Deanland Wood Park staged a number of events including a flying display by a Spitfire. On the 6th, a more formal event was held at the present airfield. Many of the visitors flew in on the day with eventually 35 aircraft arriving. This included representatives of the Tiger Club who preceded their landing with a fly past. At the commemoration, a painting showing the various squadron insignia, was unveiled by Air Chief Marshal Sir Neil Wheeler, G.C.B., C.B.E., D.F.C., A.F.C., and presented to Ripe Parish Church where it now hangs. This was followed by a Service of Remembrance and then the planting of an oak tree, in front of which was placed a plaque in memory of those pilots killed while serving at Deanland. The event was concluded by a fly past of the Lancaster, Hurricane and Spitfire of the Battle of Britain Memorial Flight.

Since then eight further small hangers have been constructed. The recent trend is for smaller light aircraft (l.s.a's) to be kept at the airfield. From 2002 to 2010 the airfield was used by the Sussex Police as a Forward Operating Base for it's helicopters. They continue to use it for occasional fire arms training. There has also been an increase in use for helicopters bringing in visitors to the Festival Season at Glyndebourne Opera.

A more recent 'battle' fought from here has been against a proposed Land Raise site immediately to the north of the airfield. The proposal has now been withdrawn, hopefully for ever. One possible benefit is that the airfield is now formally recognised by East Sussex County Council as an 'Historical Site'.

Surely, the final word must go to the pilots who still fly into Deanland airfield. Recent comments sum up the general feeling. "Flew into Deanland yesterday, a lovely grass strip in the South of England with a slight hump at the 06 end". "Very well maintained airfield and very tidy, easy to spot but plenty of areas to keep away from".

APPENDIX 1

SQUADRON DETAILS
131 POLISH AIRFIELD
No. 84 Group 2nd TAF

SQN. NUMBER:	302		
NAME:	Posnan		
MOTTO:	-		
AIRCRAFT FLOWN:	Spitfire Mk. IX	AIRCRAFT CODE: WX	
DATE FORMED:	13.7.1940	DISBANDED: 18.12.1946	
SQN. LEADER	Marian Duryasz K.W. D.F.C.		
DATES AT DEANLAND	1.4.1944 to 26.4.1944		
ARRIVED FROM:	Northolt	DEPARTED TO: Chailey	
NOTES:	Posted to Southend on 12th April for training, to return to Deanland on 14th April.		

SQN. NUMBER:	308	
NAME:	Krakow (City of Krakow)	
MOTTO:	-	
AIRCRAFT FLOWN:	Spitfire Mk. IX	AIRCRAFT CODE: ZF
DATE FORMED:	9.9.1940	DISBANDED: 18.12 1946
SQN. LEADER	Captain Witold Rettinger	
DATES AT DEANLAND	1.4.1944 to 28.4.1944	
ARRIVED FROM:	Northolt	DEPARTED TO: Chailey

SQN. NUMBER:	317	
NAME:	Wilen (City of Wilno)	
MOTTO:	-	
AIRCRAFT FLOWN:	Spitfire Mk. IX	AIRCRAFT CODE: JH
DATE FORMED:	22.4.1941	DISBANDED: 18.12.1946
SQN. LEADER	Marian Chelmecki K.W.	
DATES AT DEANLAND	1.4.1944 to 26.4.1944	
ARRIVED FROM:	Northolt	DEPARTED TO: Chailey

Additional notes

Operation Bodenplatte, mounted on 1st January 1945, was the Luftwaffes last attempt to regain air superiority. Co-ordinated attacks were mounted on all the RAF airfields on the newly re-captured mainland of Europe. No's 308 and 317 Squadron aircraft, returning from an early morning sortie, trounced the Me 109s attacking their airfield at St Denis Westrem, destroying twenty two of the German aircraft. No. 302 Squadron was unlucky. They arrived back from their dawn mission at the wrong moment, being in the process of landing as the German aircraft attacked. Nine Spitfires of No. 302 Squadron were destroyed on the ground. No. 308 Squadron was to lose seven of their aircraft with a further four damaged. No. 317 Squadron was also to lose seven of their aircraft with one other damaged.

149 AIRFIELD
No. 11 Group ADGB

SQN. NUMBER: 64
NAME: none
MOTTO: Tenax propositi (Firmness in Purpose)
AIRCRAFT FLOWN: Spitfire Mk.Vc AIRCRAFT CODE: SH
DATE FORMED: 1916-1919 REFORMED 1.3.1939
  DISBANDED 15.6.1967
SQN. LEADER John Noble MacKenzie D.F.C.
DATES AT DEANLAND 29.4.1944 to 26.6.1944
ARRIVED FROM: Bolt Head DEPARTED TO: Harrowbeer
NOTES: Converted to Mustangs in November 1944

SQN. NUMBER: 234
NAME: Madras Presidency
MOTTO: Ignem mortemque despuima (We spit fire and death)
AIRCRAFT FLOWN: Spitfire Mk. HF VI AIRCRAFT CODE: AZ
DATE FORMED: 1918-15.5.1919 REFORMED: 30.10.1939
  DISBANDED: 15.7.1957
SQN. LEADER Phil Arnott D.F.C.
DATES AT DEANLAND 29.4.1944 to 19.6.1944
ARRIVED FROM: Bolt Head DEPARTED TO: Predannack
NOTES: Played a major part in the Battle of Britain.

SQN. NUMBER: 611
NAME: West Lancashire (Auxiliary Air Force)
MOTTO: Beware, beware.
AIRCRAFT FLOWN: Spitfire Mk. LF Vb AIRCRAFT CODE: FY
DATE FORMED: 10.2.1936 DISBANDED: 10.3.1957
SQN. LEADER W.A.Douglas D.F.C.
DATES AT DEANLAND 30.4.1944 to 24.6.1944
ARRIVED FROM: Coltishall DEPARTED TO: Harrowbeer
NOTES: On 28.10.1939 was responsible for bringing down a Heinkel
  He111 near Heddington, the first enemy aircraft to be
  brought down on British soil since 1918.

No.85 Group 2ⁿᵈ TAF

SQN. NUMBER:	91
NAME:	Nigeria (Jim Crow)
MOTTO:	We seek alone.
AIRCRAFT FLOWN:	Spitfire Mk. XIV, late August changed to Mk. IXb
AIRCRAFT CODE:	DL
DATE FORMED:	1.9.1917 to 3.7.1919 REFORMED: 11.1.1941
	DISBANDED: 31.1.1947
SQN. LEADER	Norman Arthur Kynaston, killed 15.8.1944, then P.M.Bond
DATES AT DEANLAND	21.7.1944 to 7.10.1944
ARRIVED FROM:	West Malling DEPARTED TO: Biggin Hill
NOTES:	Named Nigeria after the number of subscriptions received from Nigeria for the building of Spitfires. Individual aircraft were named after provinces of Nigeria. The squadron was nicknamed Jim Crows due to their role of carrying out coastal reconnaissance patrols.

SQN. NUMBER:	322
NAME:	Dutch
MOTTO:	Neit praten maar doen (Action, not words)
AIRCRAFT FLOWN:	Spitfire Mk.XIV, late August changed to Mk. LF IXE
AIRCRAFT CODE:	VL and 3W
DATE FORMED:	12.6.1943 DISBANDED: 7.10 1945
SQN. LEADER	Mjr. K.C.Kuhlmann DFC, baled out over France and captured 1.9.1944, then C.M.van Eedenborg
DATES AT DEANLAND	21.7.1944 to 10.10.1944
ARRIVED FROM:	West Malling DEPARTED TO: Fairwood Common
NOTES:	Carried out day bomber raids and armed reconnaissance. The Squadron mascot was a parrot.

SQN. NUMBER:	345
NAME:	Free French (GC II/2 Berry)
MOTTO:	Nil actum credo si quid supersii agendum (I think nothing done if anything remains undone).
AIRCRAFT FLOWN:	Spitfire Mk. Vb, 6th September changed to Mk. HF IX
AIRCRAFT CODE:	2Y. Apparently, the squadron adopted French roundels and fin flashes in September 1944 and that no squadron code letters were used after this date.
DATE FORMED:	12.2.1944 DISBANDED: 27.11.1945
SQN. LEADER	Cm. Jean-Marie Accart
DATES AT DEANLAND	16.8.1944 to 10.10.1944
ARRIVED FROM:	Shoreham DEPARTED TO: Fairwood Common
NOTES:	When disbanded, the squadron returned to French control.

APPENDIX 2

The Spitfires of Deanland

Mk. V

More Mk.V Spitfires were built than any other version. Developed in 1941 from the Mk.II airframe, it was powered by a Rolls-Royce Merlin 45 engine with a three bladed airscrew. The B version was armed with two 20mm Hispano cannons and four 0.303 Browning machine guns. The C versions had a universal wing with a choice of guns plus the facility to carry two 250lb bombs. The LF designation indicated the aircraft had clipped wings. This variant was developed for low altitude flying.

Flown by	No. 64 Squadron Mk.VC	Sept 1943 – June 1944
	No. 345 Squadron Mk.VB	Mar 1944 – Sept 1944
	No. 611 Squadron Mk. LF VB	July 1943 – July 1944

Mk. VI

This was a modified Mk.V airframe with a Merlin 47 engine, the first with a four bladed airscrew. The majority had a B type wing armament. The HF version with it's long pointed wings, were designed for high flying.

Flown by	No.234 Squadron Mk. HF VI	Jan 1943 – Sept 1944

Mk. IX

The Mk.IX version was hurriedly developed to counter the much superior performance of FW190s at high altitude. Again a modified Mk.V airframe was used with an assortment of wing designs: LF (low altitude, clipped wing), F (standard wing) and HF (high altitude, extended wing). Different Merlin engines were fitted according to wing design. Armament designated E type was two 20mm Hispano cannons and two 0.5 Browning machine guns.

Flown by	No. 302 Squadron Mk IX	Sept 1943 – May 1944
	No. 308 Squadron Mk IX	Nov 1943 – Mar 1945
	No. 317 Squadron Mk IX	Sept 1943 – May1945
	No. 91 Squadron Mk. LF IX B	Aug 1944 – Jan 1945
	No. 322 Squadron Mk. LF IX E	Aug 1944 – Nov 1944
	No. 64 Squadron Mk. HF IX	Sept 1944 – Nov 1944

Mk. XIV

The airframe for this mark had to be considerably modified to take the new Griffon engine, the aircraft being three foot longer than previous models. The Mk.65 and 66 engines were fitted with five bladed airscrews. Armament was either B or E type, the cannons now being the Mk.2 Hispano series. Heavy but powerful, these Spitfires were challenging to maintain. The engine exhausts quickly burnt away and the tyres needed to be often changed because of the heavy operating weight.

Flown by	No. 91 Squadron Mk. XIV	Mar 1944 – Aug 1944
	No. 322 Squadron Mk. XIV	Mar 1944 – Aug 1944

The cost of a Spitfire in 1939.

Fuselage	£2,500	Rolls-Royce Merlin Engine £2000	
Wings	£1,800 a pair	Guns	£800
Undercarriage	£800	Propeller	£350
Clock	£2.10s	Spark plugs	8s each
TOTAL	Around £9,500 each		

Pilots comments on the Spitfire.

'She was a perfect lady, she had no vices.'

'She was beautifully positive. You could dive till your eyes were popping out of your head and she would still answer to a touch.'

'She could outmanoeuvre German aircraft with it's immensely strong wings.'

'The one I liked best was the clipped and cropped Spit. I really loved it because it had a super rate of roll and you could really pull it in.'

'The Spitfire LFVb was a delightful aeroplane to fly for the purpose it had been modified – low-level combat with the Focke-Wulf Fw 190.'

APPENDIX 3
Specification for Deanland ALG
As recorded on Air Ministry plan 585/44 February 1944

Ref	No	Building	Remark
1	2	Runways	1600yrds x 1400yrds
2		Perimeter track	35ft army track co square
3	30	Aircraft dispersal standings	
4		Access track to aircraft dispersal stand	
5		-	
6	4	Blister hangers	
7			
8	40	SAA stores 100'x100'	In four groups of 10 sights at aircraft disposal
8a	20	SAA stores	On one group around dispersal
8b	4	Piro stores	Two at one flight group of 15
			One " " " 15
			One " " " 6
8c	1	Piro stores	Central dump
9	4	Refueling points 200'x100'	Also used as aircraft dispersal
10	1	Petrol installation	24,000 gallons
11	1	Oil storage 54'x54'	Hard core compound with wire fence enclosure
12	1	MT Petrol	Barn at Broomham Farm to be used
13	1	Paraffin Store	Hardcore compound with wire fence enclosure sited on communal stores
14	1	Fuel compound 54'x54'	End as 13
15	1	MT standing	To be provided along access road to Broomham Farm
16	1	HQ Office & PBx	To be provided in Broomham Farm
17	1	Squadron Office & Messing Room	To be provided in Broomham Farm
18	1	Armoury	To be provided on ground floor of Cleggetts Farm House
19	1	Main Store	Barn and outbuildings of Cleggetts Farm to be used

20	1	Ration Store	Sited on communal area
21	2	Water Storage	Sited on communal area
22	3	Ablution Blocks	Shelters sited on communal area
23	3	Latrines(sleeping qtrs)	One on each site
23a	4	Latrines (aircraft dispersal)	
23b	1	Latrine (technical area)	
23c	3	Latrines (communal)	One for officers, one for other ranks
24	1	Sullage tank	
25		Electricity supply	To provide charging
26		MI & Crash room	Not required
27	3	Air raid shelters – slit types	One 84ft, two 72ft long
27a	8	Air raid shelters – communal area	Each shelter 120 ft long
27b	4	Air raid shelters – technical area	Each shelter 49ft long
27c	7	Air raid shelters – aircraft dispersal	Each shelter 60ft long
28		Access	
29	2	Hard standing for cooking	25 x25
30	3	Footpaths to sleeping quarters	
	9	Sleeping sites	
	Requisitioned properties "Broadacres" –to be used for officers quarters "Cleggetts Farm" – Upper floor for officers & sergeants quarters. For ground floor see armoury.		
	If ground conditions do not permit slit type shelters – banked up above ground blast protection is to be provided.		

APPENDIX 4

Other Local Airfields

Eastbourne Airfield at St Antony's Hill and Seaplane base and factory at the Crumbles

Opened   December 1911   Closed December 1920
Used by   Eastbourne Flying School, Eastbourne Aviation Company.
St Antony's Hill was requisitioned by the RNAS during the 1914-1918 war and became one of the most important RNAS flying schools in the country.
Aircraft built at Eastbourne   BE 2C, Avro 504A, Avro 504K

Polegate Airship Station
Opened   July 1915   Closed 1919
Used by   RNAS Dover Command
Flying   SS type airship, SS Zero type airship

Telscombe Home Defence Landing Ground
Opened   November 1916   Closed February 1919
Used by   No.78 and No.242 Squadrons
Flying   BE 2C & BE12 Biplanes and DH 6.

Wilmington Home Defence Landing Ground, later a civil airport.
Opened   1916   Closed Sept 1939
Used by   Sussex Aero Club and later Eastbourne Flying Club
Flying   De Havilland 60G Moths

Newhaven RNAS Seaplane Station
Opened   May 1917   Closed Sept 1920
Used by   408 & 409 Flights
Flying   Short 184 Floatplanes, Dover 184 Floatplanes,
   Fairey Compania 111B Seaplanes

Friston Forward Satellite Airfield
Opened   July 1940   Closed April 1946
Used by   Nos.253, 32, 402, 412, 41, 610 Squadrons
   Nos.349, 350 (Belgian) Squadrons
   No. 316 (Polish Squadron)
Flying   Spitfire Vb, XII, XIV, Hurricane, Mustang 111S, Lysander, Auster